Carolyn Miller's
Sportacular Warmups
Book Two

Foreword

The purpose of this series is to increase the student's technical ability. Each book contains material designed to strengthen fingers, increase flexibility, and help the student master the many technical skills needed to perform. *Sportacular Warmups* combines sports and music. Students can relate the musical exercise to a similar activity in the five sport areas. At the end of each section there is a solo that is made up of exercises from that section. This is a wonderful review.

I hope your students will enjoy *Sportacular Warmups* and will become "Sportacular" pianists!

Carolyn Miller

Contents

©MCMXCVIII by The Willis Music Company
International Copyright Secured
printed in the USA

I.
BASKETBALL

1. Dribbling

2. Traveling

3. Basket

4. Time Clock

5. Over and Back

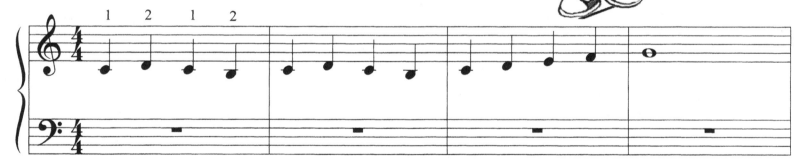

6. Tip In

7. Nothing But Net
(Swoosh!)

8. Jump Shot

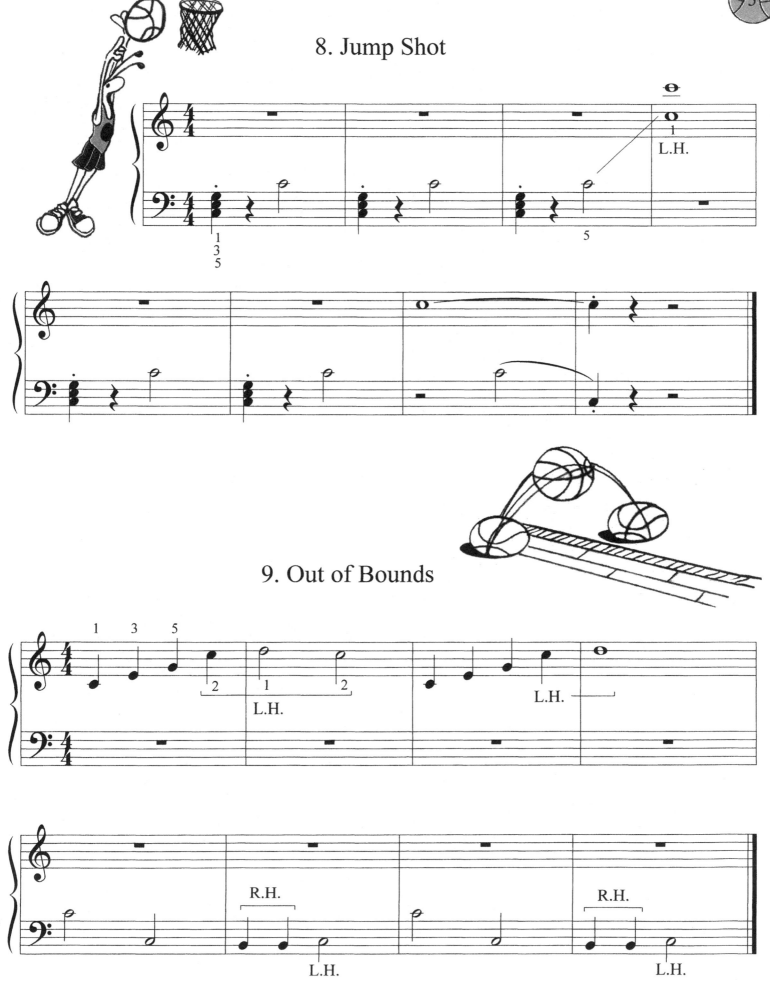

9. Out of Bounds

10. Lay Up

11. Walking

12. Division Finals

II.
BASEBALL

1. Stretching

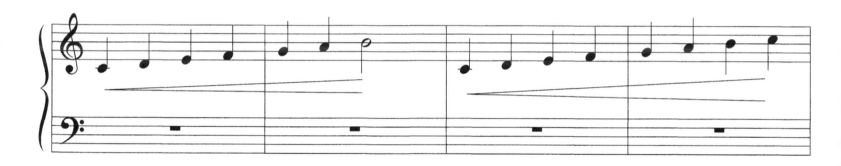

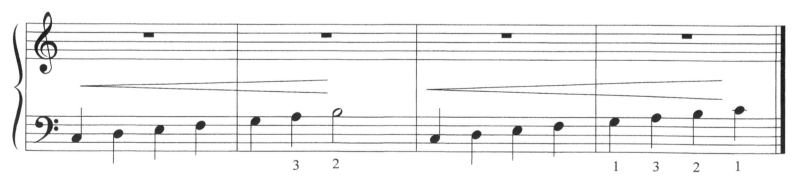

2. Curve Ball

3. Bunt

4. Rundown

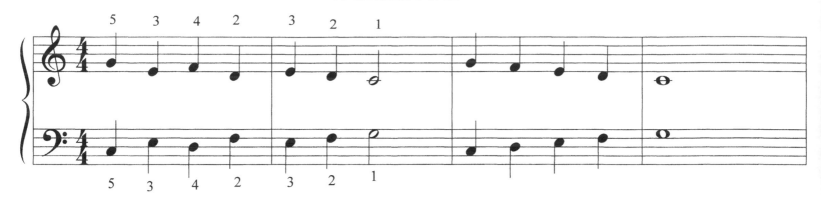

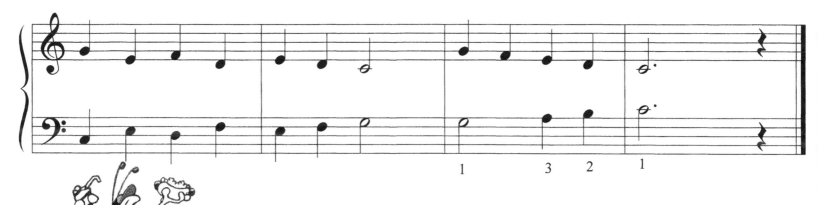

5. Take Me Out to the Ball Game

6. Seventh Inning Stretch

7. Error

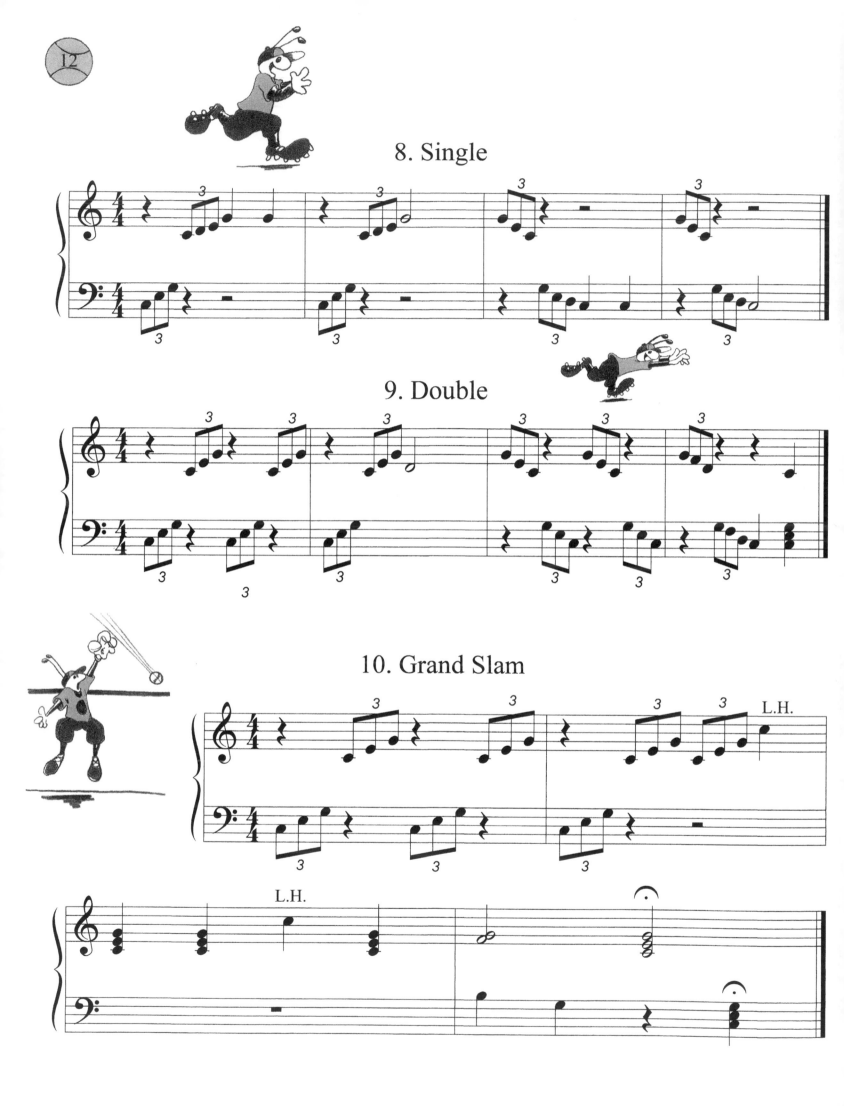

8. Single

9. Double

10. Grand Slam

11. All-Star Game

III.
TRACK AND FIELD

1. Jumping Rope on Alternating Feet

2. Jumping Rope on Two Feet

3. Pole Vault

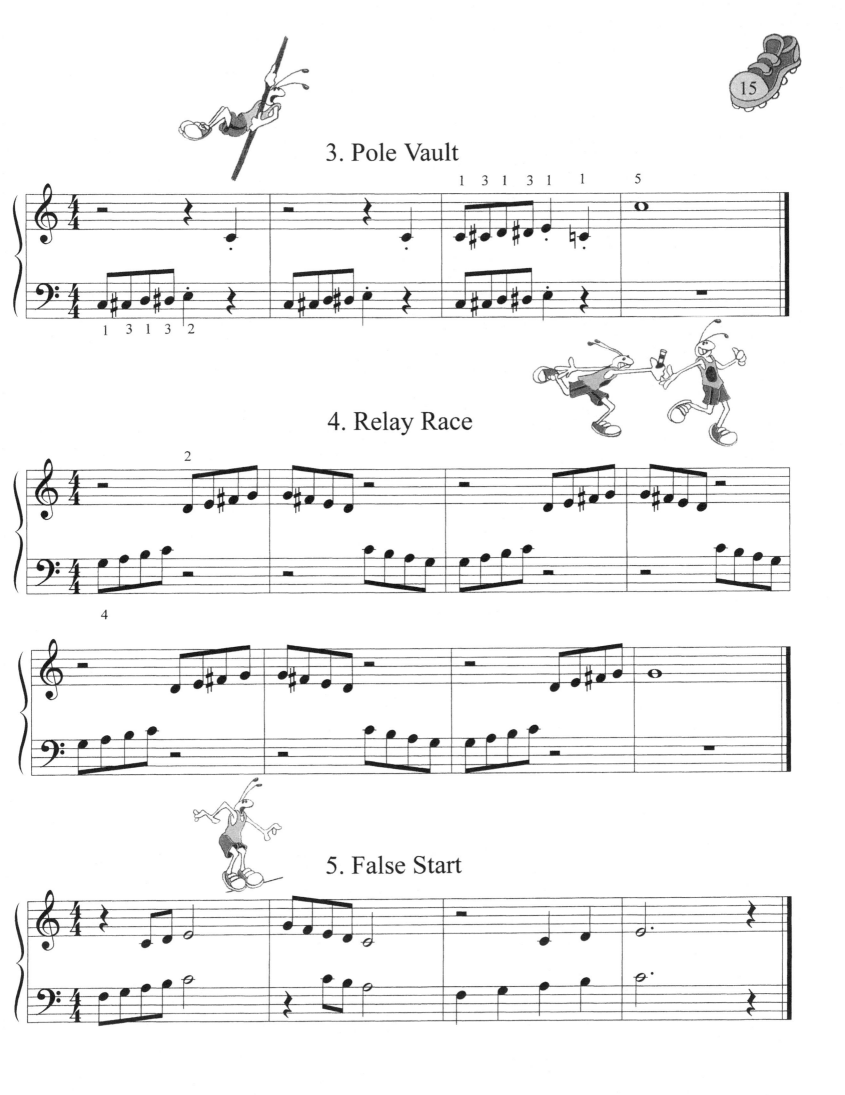

4. Relay Race

5. False Start

6. Flexibility

7. On Your Mark, get set, and Go!

8. Three Laps

9. Photo Finish

10. Go for the Gold!

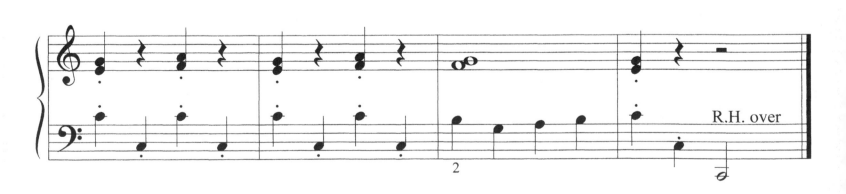

R.H. over

19

11. State Finals

IV.
EXTREME ADVENTURE SPORTS

1. Climbing Up the Mountain

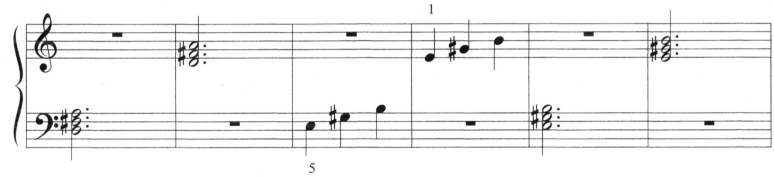

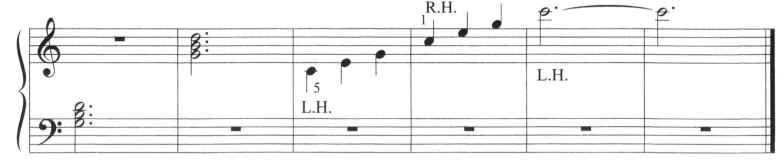

2. Free Fall

3. Belay On

4. Rowing

5. Rowing
(Danger Ahead)

6. Bungee Jumping

7. Wheelie

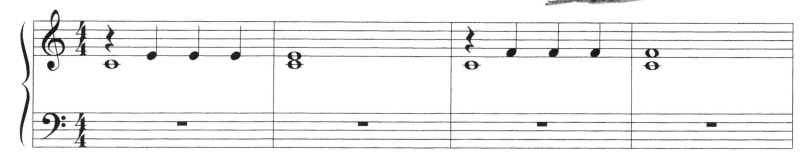

8. Rollerblading

9. Take the Challenge

V.
SOCCER

1. Direct Kick

2. Back Header

3. Tripping

4. Dribbling

5. Faster Dribbling

6. Cross

7. Juggling

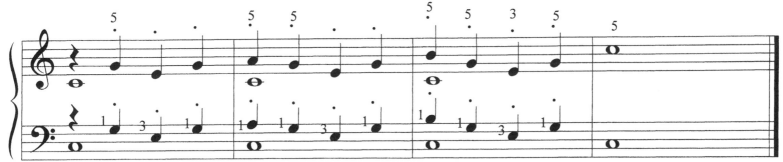

8. Penalty Kick

9. Goal

10. Semi-finals

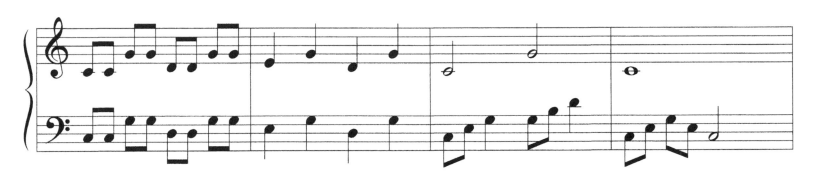

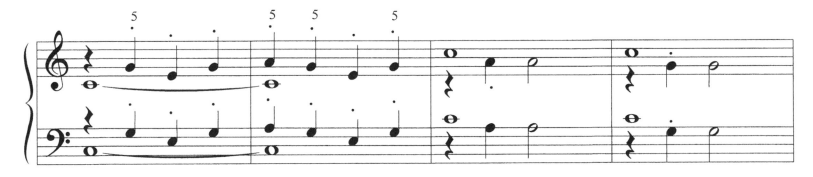

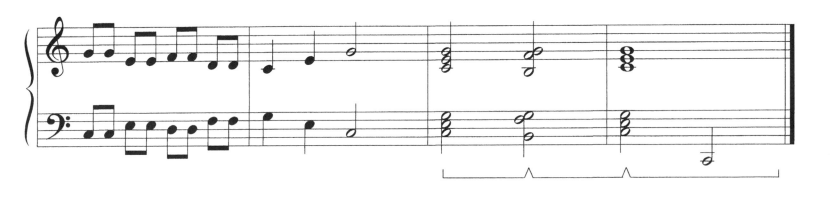